LIONEL MESSI

THE BOY WHO DREAMED OF BEING A CHAMPION

AN ARGENTINIAN BOY'S TALE OF GRIT, TALENT, AND TRIUMPH

Dedication

To Gloria:

Thank you for the infinte wisdom and spoils.

"They tell me all men are equal in God's eyes, Messi makes you seriously think about those words."

Ray Hudson

Before you start

This book is produced with ❤️ for children everywhere in the USA.

As it was originally written for a global audience, you will find that we call soccer "football" throughout the book.

Please know that we mean soccer in those instances - the same beautiful game that unites us all.

Table of contents

Introduction

People will forever debate who the best football player of all time is.

The likes of Pelé, Marta, Ronaldo, Hamm and Maradona will always be in the mix - often trading places at the top of everyone's list.

People who *really* know football will tell you that there is only one player who is The Greatest of All Time.

His story is a story of incredible determination and resilience, of sadness and despair, but ultimately, one that ends in eternal glory.

CHILDHOOD

The Revered Rosarian

Lionel Andrés Messi was born on the 24th of June 1987 in Rosario, Argentina.

Both his parents worked in factories. His dad in a steel factory and his mom in a magnet one. Even though they both worked very hard, Lionel's parents didn't have a lot of money. It was tough for them to support Lionel, his two older brothers, and his younger sister.

There was one thing however, that the whole family LOVED. It was the one thing that always united them and brought them incredible happiness. And this was football.

It was because of this love, and together with his older brothers, that Messi started playing football at a very young age. By the age of four he was playing for Grandoli Football Club where he was coached by his father.

Even at four years old, he stood out. It was clear that Messi had a special talent for football!

At six years old, he started playing for Newell's Old Boys, and it was on those dusty Rosario football pitches that the young boy started catching everyone's eye. Every week he would be seen dancing his way past opponents, ball glued to his feet, before unleashing rockets into the back of different nets.

Incredibly, most of these opponents were children who were older and much bigger than him! But that didn't phase Lionel, he scored a few hundred goals in his short time at Newell's.

His parents never really worried about him being small either. After all, it would only be a matter of time before he caught up in height with the rest of his peers.

Four years passed however, and despite improving as a player, young Lionel never really caught up in height to his teammates. It was at this stage where he suffered one of the biggest disappointments of his life.

Left Stunned

When Leo (that was the nickname that would stick for the rest of his life) was 10 years old, the doctors gave him some terrible news. They said he had a "growth hormone deficiency".

Slightly confused, he asked his parents to explain what that meant.

Sadly, it meant that his body wasn't going to grow to be the same height as the rest of his friends and of people his age. He would forever be a lot shorter than everyone else.

The only way to fix this was to take special pills that would make him grow "normally".

Young Leo was only 10, but already he was showing he was mentally very strong and determined by agreeing to take these pills.

What Leo didn't know was that these pills were incredibly expensive, and his parents were really struggling to be able to afford them. His dad asked Newell's to pay for the pills but the club said no.

In the year 2000, Argentina as a country hit a financial crisis (a financial crisis is where everyone in the country struggles to get money) and his parents could no longer afford the pills.

As they had relatives in Barcelona in Spain, they did everything they could to get Barcelona Football Club to arrange a trial for young Leo.

They were hopeful that Leo would impress them so much that the club would sign him. If that happened, they hoped that Barcelona would pay for his special pills.

In the end, his parents did manage to arrange a trial, and at just 13 years of age, Lionel Messi flew to Spain.

A King Born on a Napkin

Once in Spain, Messi first played in front of Barcelona for a man called Charly Rexach. Rexach was a scout in charge bringing younger players through to the famous Barça youth academy: La Masia.

Rexach was very impressed when he saw Messi play, he wanted to sign him straight away!

However, at the time it was really unusual for clubs to sign foreign players at such a young age. Rexach's hands were tied - his bosses simply wouldn't make a move for Messi.

After three months of waiting for Barcelona to make a decision, Leo's dad had enough! He said that if Barcelona didn't sign him, he would take his son back to Argentina.

Rexach couldn't waste this opportunity - he knew Leo was one in a million, maybe even *billion* - and he couldn't afford for this young talent to leave Barcelona. In one instinctive move, he picked up the napkin in front of him, scribbled a short contract on it, and on behalf of his club (brave move!) offered it to Lionel and his dad.

Leo's dad took one look at the napkin. That piece of paper would guarantee that his son's expensive growth treatment would be paid for by the club.

Without hesitation, he signed the napkin and Messi was officially enrolled in the world's most famous football academy: La Masia.

He would start in three months - and that was enough time for his mom, brothers and sister to move from Argentina and come join him in Spain.

Heartbreak For Barças's Future Hero

Things in Spain could not have started worse for Leo.

Due to an argument with his old club Newell's and his new club Barcelona, he wasn't allowed to play in any game that wasn't a friendly.

That meant that he didn't really feel like he was fitting in with his new football friends. Whilst all his teammates were playing in every game, he would only be allowed to play a handful of those.

This obviously had an impact on him. His teammates Cesc Fábregas and Gerard Piqué would describe him as being very shy (on top of being very tiny too!).

Some teammates claimed that he was so shy that they thought he was mute!

If Messi felt sad off the pitch, then on it he was anything but sad. It was on the football field that he became alive, and for those wondering whether he was a mute, it was on the football pitch that he did his "talking".

By this point, everyone was starting to take note of this young new phenomenon at La Masia.

But as things were looking up on the football field, he suffered yet another setback.

His mom, brothers and sister didn't like Barcelona, so they decided to go back to Argentina. They left Leo and his dad on their own in Spain and Leo constantly missed them.

For all the great things he was doing every few days for 90 minutes, the rest of the time he felt tremendously homesick. It would have been easy to just go back to Argentina.

But as the famous saying goes, when the going gets tough, the tough get going. And that is exactly what Leo did.

JOURNEY TO GERMANY 2006

Ferocious Fighting For His Family

From the ages of 13 to 16 Leo gave his heart and soul on football pitches around Catalonia (that's the area of Spain that Barcelona is in).

He felt that was the least he could do for his family as they had sacrificed so many things for him.

Messi knew that the reason why half of his family was in Argentina and the other half in Spain was because of the love they had for him, and the belief that one day he would accomplish his dream of becoming a professional footballer.

Within a year of his family leaving, Leo had finished his growth treatment. He had also sorted out the legal disputes with Newell's and found himself playing in every game for Barcelona.

In three short years he progressed up the Barcelona club structure from:

Cadetes A
> Juveniles B
>> Juveniles A
>>> Barcelona C
>>>> Barcelona B

When Leo was only 16 years old, Frank Rijkaard had seen enough.

Frank Rijkaard was the Head Coach of Barcelona FC, and he invited him to come and train with the Barcelona A Team.

Football Family

As a young Leo stepped into Barcelona's dressing room, he was met with some of the biggest names in the history of football.

In his debut season he would share a dressing room with the likes of Carles Puyol, Samuel Eto'o, Xavi Hernández, Rafael Márquez, and none other than the biggest global superstar (and probably best player in the world at the time) Ronaldinho.

Messi had always been a quiet person. He liked to keep himself to himself so he didn't really talk much to anyone.

All the Barcelona superstars were wondering whether he had what it took to become a world class player. How could someone so quiet and shy deliver on the world's biggest football stage?

Once again, Leo did his talking by playing football.

One of the Barcelona superstars, Ludovic Giuly, described Leo as an "alien". He was so good that he had to be out of this world.

Giuly later described how a 16 year old Leo "destroyed" all the first team players in training. He would continuously dribble past all of them on the way to scoring goal after goal.

The first team players were so angry that a little boy was doing this to them that they would kick Leo to the ground to stop him from getting past them. Leo would simply, get up, dust himself off, and do it all over again. All without saying a word.

After the initial anger subsided, the players couldn't help but realize how lucky they were. Yes, they were being embarrassed by a young boy, but this young boy played for their team. Imagine what he would do to opposing teams?!

So, after only the first training session, and led by Ronaldinho, the whole team took it upon themselves to wrap their arms around their "younger brother".

Leo had found another loving family.

unicef
unicef

Debut Delight

Leo played a friendly for the Barcelona A team when he was 16 years old. He had an impressive game and excited all his teammates.

Despite the promising performance, manager Frank Rijkaard kept him playing for the reserves for another year.

This was probably because Ronaldinho (the world's greatest player at the time) played in Barcelona as a left winger - which was Messi's position too.

However, it wasn't long before Rijkaard succumbed to the constant pressure from the senior players to bring Messi into the team, and on October 16 2004, Messi made his official debut for Barcelona.

At 17 years old - technically still not even an adult - and with 8 minutes remaining in a game against Espanyol, he became the youngest player ever to play for the Barcelona senior team.

This boy's dream had *just* come true.

All of the sacrifices he and his family had made - the tears, the distance, the legal battles, the growth therapy - they all finally paid off the moment he high fived Deco and made his way onto the pitch that late autumn evening in 2004.

It was the beginning of the greatest career the world of football would ever see...

DECO

Breaking Through

For the remainder of the 2004 to 2005 season Messi would come on as a substitute and have an impact on the tiring legs of opposing teams.

He was only getting 10 to 20 minutes per game - remember that at this stage he was still technically a boy amongst men - but leaving a huge footprint on games.

It was around this point that his new nickname was born. People were starting to refer to this new phenomenal football player as Lionel "La Pulga" Messi. "La Pulga" is Spanish for "The Flea" - a reference to how small he was.

Messi had only gone and turned around his height disadvantage, the very same one that had almost cost him his career, to make it his biggest threat.

With his low center of gravity and incredible speed, he was causing havoc in opposing defenses and making incredible impacts during games.

One of the biggest impacts would come on May 1 2005 against Albacete.

Ronaldinho, who had taken it upon himself to be the biggest of the "Barcelona Big Brothers" to Messi, received a ball from La Pulga close to the area.

As two defenders quickly closed down all his passing options, he cleverly scooped the ball over their heads. Messi read the situation beautifully, and after letting the ball bounce once, he delicately lobbed the ball over the oncoming keeper. GOOOAALL!

A beautiful one at that, and the first of hundreds for Barcelona!

Messi would quickly go on to cement his place in the starting 11 of Barcelona, winning the league title in 2005.

In 2006, he suffered one of his biggest professional setbacks: An injury ruled him out of the Champions League final. Luckily for him, Barcelona still managed to beat Arsenal in Paris in that final and he earned a Champion League winners medal.

World Cup Weight

Just as Leo was starting to overcome all the setbacks that had plagued him as a young boy, a big storm started to brew.

This was barely a year into being an adult, and it would bring dark clouds that would linger over his head for more than 15 years.

The storm would come in the way of the pressure that all Argentinians would put on his shoulders.

You see, Argentina is one of the best countries in the world at football. And by 2006 they had gone 20 years without winning the World Cup, which is far too long for a country that has constantly produced some of the world's best footballers.

The last time that they had won the World Cup it had been due to a certain Diego Maradona. He was one of the greatest ever football players, and he single handedly dismantled teams in 1986 on the way to lifting the most coveted trophy in football history.

Argentinians really wanted to win the World Cup again, more than anything in the world! And in Leo they saw someone who was as good as Diego Maradona, so they immediately demanded that he also dismantle other teams on the way to World Cup victory.

This expectation was incredibly hard to handle for Leo. Imagine carrying the dreams and aspirations of 40 million people? And poor Leo was still only a teenager!

Leo performed well at the 2006 World Cup and even scored a goal. It was because of that that everyone was very confused when his manager didn't play him when Argentina faced Germany.

Germany would eliminate Argentina that day, and Messi, with the expectations of 40 million Argentineans on his shoulders, couldn't do a single thing about it. His manager left him on the bench for the duration of the game.

He cut a desolate figure on the bench that day.

SUPER POWERS TO SOUTH AFRICA 2010

First Copa America Appearance

The Copa America is a competition played between all the countries in the South American continent.

After the World Cup, it is the second most wanted trophy by Argentineans across the world. This is because winning it usually means getting one over their arch rivals Brazil, who usually have the best players in the world.

In 2007 Argentina got to the final of the Copa America, and faced none other than Brazil in that game.

Having had a great tournament and with a few goals to his name, Leo was confident that he would help Argentina to Copa America glory.

Unfortunately for him, Brazil beat Argentina in the final 3-0. Leo was distraught.

He was inconsolable when the full time whistle went.

He had been so close to winning a tournament with Argentina, before victory had been cruelly taken away from him.

At just 20 years old, he was experiencing one of the worst feelings in his life: A defeat for his country in a major final. Sadly, it wouldn't be the only one in his career.

Leo being Leo, he didn't feel like it was just *his* loss. He felt responsible for the loss of 40 million football-loving people in his home country.

Being named the best young player of the tournament didn't really mean anything to him. He *really* wanted to win a trophy for the people of Argentina.

Olympic Honor

Fortunately for Leo, he didn't have to wait long to win a major international tournament with Argentina.

Unluckily for him perhaps, it was a tournament that many people believe isn't that big a tournament in the football world.

The Olympic Games come round once every four years. It is the oldest competition in the world and it dates back a few thousand years. Amongst many different sports and disciplines, it highlights the very best of human sacrifice in order to become the very best at what they do.

Ask any athlete who isn't a footballer, and that is THE prize they want to win.

In this prestigious tournament in Beijing in 2008, Leo had an incredible few weeks. He scored two goals and assisted two others en route to winning the whole tournament and claiming an Olympic gold medal!

Despite the initial happiness from the people of Argentina, not a huge fuss was made about this achievement.

The Football World taught a young Leo a lesson that day: That unless he won one of the "Big Two" (the World cup or Copa America) he wasn't going to be recognized as a great player.

What was even more of a setback for Leo was that as a result of winning an international tournament for Argentina, the whole country now put even more pressure on him to win a tournament "that mattered".

In the race to win the hearts of the Argentinian people, Leo started feeling as if he was destined to lose no matter what...

Rocketing to Royalty Status

Coming back as Olympic champion had a massive effect on Leo's club career.

This was the time when Leo went from being a great football player, to arguably the best in the world - and it all stemmed from a change in management at Barcelona FC.

Pep Guardiola became manager and he revolutionized the sport. He made it a more high tempo, high pressing, high energy kind of game.

At the heart of this revolution was Lionel Messi, still only 21 years old, who was quickly becoming everyone's favorite player on Earth.

By the end of the domestic season, Barcelona had won the Spanish Cup and the Spanish League, with Messi scoring 23 goals in the league to guide them to success.

One game remained in their season for them to achieve something that had never been achieved in the history of Spanish football, and that was to win "The Treble" (The Spanish League, The Spanish Cup and the Champions League).

In Rome in 2009, Barcelona faced European champions Manchester United in the final of the Champions League to decide who would be Champions of Europe.

With Barça leading 1-0, Messi rose high in the air after a cross was lobbed into the area. It was at this moment in time that all the childhood worries about his growth deficiency disappeared.

In an instant they became a thing of the past as he towered higher than 6"2 defender Rio Ferdinand and headed the ball into the back of the net.

Barcelona won The Treble that evening and "La Pulga" officially established himself as a force to be reckoned with for the next 15 years.

MESSI
10
AIG
5

The Decade of The GOATs

In 2009 Leo won his first Ballon D'or. This is a yearly award that is given to the best footballer in the world.

2009 would also mark the beginning of one of the biggest rivalries in the history of any sport - let alone football.

A certain Cristiano Ronaldo was also flourishing at the same time as Lionel Messi, and between them they would go on to win all but one Ballon D'ors between 2008 and 2021.

Never before had football seen two of the all time greatest compete at the same time and in the same league. There was a healthy rivalry between Ronaldo and Messi throughout those years - a sight to behold for lovers of football around the world.

A rivalry that would see them both push themselves to incredulous highs, but one that, if measured by Ballon D'ors, Messi undoubtedly won.

In that time, Messi was voted the best player in the world a record 7 times. Ronaldo won that award "only" 5 times.

It would seem that it was clear to everyone that Messi was the best player on Earth.

However, as far as history books went, and especially in the minds of Argentinians, that would never really be confirmed unless he mirrored Maradona's achievement of winning a World Cup.

And so it was that in 2010, with Maradona as manager of Argentina and Messi as playmaker-in-chief, that Argentinians the world over were convinced that it would be the year when World Cup glory would return to Argentina.

South African Somberness

Unfortunately for Argentina, the combination of their two greatest players (one as a manager and the other as a player) didn't pay off.

One Argentinian journalist said it best when she said that Maradona thrived on conflict, whilst Messi thrived on cooperation.

This opposing approach to football from the two greats didn't quite work in South Africa, and despite Maradona handing the captain's armband to Messi for one of the games, the two saviors of Argentinian football couldn't bring football glory to their nation.

Once again, Argentina found themselves beaten by Germany. And yet again it was at the quarter final stages of the tournament - the exact same stage at which they had been beaten by the Germans four years earlier.

This time round however, they were humiliated 4-0 by the German side. It was their worst defeat in a World Cup for more than 35 years.

A result that was so embarrassing, that it would cost Maradona his job as manager, and which left many people wondering whether Messi was good enough to win a major trophy for Argentina.

After the tournament, Leo was yet again made to feel like he had let down 40 million Argentinians.

UNBEATABLE TO BRAZIL 2014

2011 Heaven

In 2011 Lionel Messi had arguably his best season at Barcelona.

He kicked off the 2010-2011 campaign by scoring a hat-trick in the Supercopa final against Sevilla.

Barcelona then went on to record 16 consecutive victories in La Liga, a record that hasn't been surpassed to this day. Needless to say, Messi won the 5th of his ten La Liga titles that season.

In the final of the Champions League, Barcelona met Manchester United, and again beat the English side by a margin of two goals. Needless to say, La Pulga found himself on the scoresheet at Wembley that night too.

Barcelona would also go on to win the European Super Cup and the FIFA Club World Cup that season. Needless to say, Leo got voted as the best player on the planet that year.

Apart from the Copa Del Rey, Messi won everything that he competed for that year.

Things surely could not get any better for him...

... or could they?

MESSI
10

2012: A Record-Breaking Year

It would have been easy for Messi to rest on his laurels after 2011. He was only 24 years old and he had already won everything there was to win at club level.

La Pulga was hungry for more though, and he kept pushing himself to unbelievable new highs.

In 2012 Messi became the first player to score 5 goals in a single Champions League game when they beat Bayern Leverkusen 7-1.

In the same year (and remember that he was still only 24 years old!) he became Barcelona's all time top scorer after scoring a hat-trick against Grananda.

By the end of the 2012 season, Messi had won the Copa Del Rey again, and finished the season with 73 goals in all competitions.

That is 73 goals in only 60 games!

On average Leo scored 1.2 goals per game in every game he played in during 2011-2012. That made him the single-season top scorer in the history of European club football.

He wouldn't slow down at the beginning of the 2012-2013 season either, and come December he broke a record that had stood for 40 years.

That was Gert Müller's record of 85 goals scored in a calendar year for club and country.

Leo scored an unbelievable 91 goals in 2012! More than anyone in the history of the sport had ever done in one calendar year.

Following that new record, he was awarded the Ballon D'or that year for the 4th time in his life.

The GOAT Rivalry Heats Up

It is very unusual for two of the all time greats to play football in the same era. Even more unusual is for them to be direct rivals in the greatest club derby in the world.

By 2012 Cristiano Ronaldo had moved from Manchester United to Real Madrid and had been impressing with the Spanish giants for a few years.

Two of the greatest players ever were facing off against each other every few months, and together they were winning everything there was on offer.

Ronaldo and Messi never became friends, but there was a healthy rivalry and respect between the two that kept pushing them both to be the absolute best.

By the end of 2014, Messi had won 4 Ballon D'Ors to Ronaldo's 3.

The two players had single handedly made the 2010's belong to Spain in terms of European trophies.

Their style of play and achievements would go on to divide the footballing world in determining *who* actually was the best. A debate that will rage on for eternity in footballing circles.

As they both had won everything at their disposal in terms of club football, it seemed as if the debate would have to be settled by who would lead their national team to more international trophies.

FIFA
BALLON
DOR
2011
Football
FIFA
BALLON
DOR
2015

Brazil Beckons

When the World Cup of 2014 was held in Brazil, Messi had already established himself as the captain of the team.

Going into the World Cup, pundits were second-guessing Messi's ability to put on a good performance during the tournament as he had been plagued with injuries.

It is very surprising that anyone would second-guess Messi's footballing ability, let alone experts.

They were simply going off the fact that messi's incredible stats in the previous months had dropped from "superhuman-and-almost-impossible-to-believe" to simply "incredibly good"

And just as he did when he was a shy teenager starting off at Barcelona, Messi responded to his critics by doing his talking on the pitch that summer.

He scored a few goals and assisted a couple of others to lead Argentina to the final of the World Cup.

Eternal glory beckoned for him at the home of Brazilian football: the Maracaná stadium.

He was one game away from winning the biggest prize in world football, and as captain, he was ready to lead the way.

No amount of pressure would stand in his quest of bringing back the most coveted trophy in the whole of Argentina.

Unfortunately for Leo, a very organized and determined German side *also* wanted that trophy badly.

In the 113th minute of their game against Argentina, they scored the solitary goal that robbed Leo of achieving the one thing he had wanted his whole life.

Germany won the World Cup that evening.

10
10

ROTTEN RUN TO RUSSIA 2018

Argentinian Anger

Messi being Messi, it only took him a year to dust himself off from the Brazilian heartache and lead his national team to another final.

Very few players ever achieve back-to-back international finals, but Leo, of course, is cut from a different cloth.

In the Copa America 2015 final they found themselves facing Chile to decide who was going to be the continent's best team.

Unfortunately for Argentina, they drew 0-0 with Chile and lost 4-1 on penalties.

What followed after that game was one of the saddest and most unfair things to have happened in Leo's life. All his adoring fans in Argentina suddenly turned on him!

Despite the incredible highs that he had given the country (finals, Olympic medals, etc.), people were coming out saying the nastiest things about him.

Argentinian people started spreading rumors about how little he loved Argentina. They said he felt more European than Argentinian and that was the reason why he achieved so much for Barcelona and so little for Argentina.

They would accuse him of being too detached from the Argentine people because he had left the country when he was 13 years old. He wasn't the "player of the people" like other teammates such as Carlos Tevez. Very hurtful stuff.

People started saying that they wanted to kill Messi - and that is when a line was crossed. It was unacceptable. Saying that is *never* OK. Not even if it's said as a joke.

The way he was being treated was outrageous and Leo felt the saddest he had ever felt. He thought that stopping playing football was the only way to protect him and his family.

He was close to quitting football.

AFA
10

Redemption Hour

Despite the whole of Argentina being mean to Leo, he continued to represent his country superbly, and once again, he led them to the Copa America final in 2016.

It was a repeat of the 2015 final against Chile, only this time it was being held in New Jersey in the USA.

This was Argentina's third major final in 3 years. And surely, as the famous saying goes, it would be third time lucky for Leo and Argentina, right?

The game against Chile finished 0-0 again! It would have to be decided on penalties.

Messi missed his penalty and Chile ended up winning 4-2.

Three final losses in a row, together with the horrible way in which he was being treated by Argentina, was too much.

A tearful Messi retired from playing international football after that game.

"I've tried my hardest and it isn't to be. A decision has been made.", Leo said. The "decision" was his retirement after failing to win a trophy with Argentina.

At only 29 years old, this sent shockwaves around the world. He was still at the peak of his superpowers!

The best player in the world saying that he was never going to play again was exactly what Argentina needed to wake up and realize how badly they had treated Leo in recent years.

Begging Back For The Best

Things changed drastically in Argentina immediately after Leo announced his retirement.

The next day various newspapers ran national campaigns asking him to reconsider his future.

Within weeks, the mayor of Buenos Aires (the capital city of Argentina) made a statue of Messi in the city to try and convince him to keep playing.

The football association of Argentina offered to organize themselves based around Leo's needs. Whatever he wanted he would get.

Even the president of Argentina got involved and sent a heartfelt message to Leo begging him to come back and play for the country.

People suddenly realized that they had mistreated him badly, and that they were obviously better off with him in the team.

Something outside of Argentina also happened that year. Something *so* big that it touched Leo in the heart: Cristiano Ronaldo single handedly led Portugal to win the European Championship.

Remember that healthy rivalry they had?

Well, that international win for Ronaldo would almost certainly have him be the GOAT (Greatest of All Time) over Messi.

Leo did *not* want that.

So, after only a few weeks of international retirement, La Pulga announced that he was reversing his decision and that he would play again for Argentina at the upcoming World Cup qualifiers for Russia 2018.

Ruined in Russia

Once again, Leo did what he did best and qualified his national team to play at the upcoming World Cup in Russia.

Frustratingly for La Pulga, Argentina struggled in the group stages and just about managed to scrape through to the second round, where they faced France in the Russian city of Kazan.

In a game which would become known as The Classic of Kazan, Argentina lost 4-3 to eventual World Cup winners France.

Leo assisted two goals in that game, but unfortunately, that wasn't enough to progress in the tournament.

Argentina had, yet again, failed in the biggest of stages.

Leo started wondering whether his coming back from retirement was worth it. After all, he kept losing with his national team.

Had all his efforts for Argentina been for nothing? It seemed as if he was never going to win anything!

Little did he know that 4 years later, he would go on to face France again at a World Cup...

Bust in Brazil

In 2019 the Copa America was played in Brazil. Argentina scraped through to the semi-finals where they faced the hosts of the tournament.

They lost 2-0 and, yet again, Leo felt destined to win nothing with his beloved Argentina.

In what could possibly be described as *some* consolation, Argentina beat Chile in the third place play off.

This was somewhat of a redemption as Argentina had lost to Chile in their last two finals.

Unfortunately for Leo, he got sent off in that game. He also made some unsavory comments about the referees which landed him in hot water.

It was clear that Leo was growing ever so frustrated with his lack of trophies for the Argentinian national team.

In fifteen years of trying to win something for Argentina, he only had one Olympic Gold medal to his name, and zero major international trophies.

He was close to breaking...

AFA
10
CL

THE ROAD TO ETERNAL GLORY
QATAR 2022

Mission Accomplished at the Maracaná

In July 2021 Leo found himself back in Brazil playing in the final of the 2021 Copa America.

The final was against the reigning champions, and hosts of the tournament: Brazil.

And it was in no other place than the spiritual home of Brazilian football: The Maracaná Stadium.

The last time Leo had been in that stadium in a final of a major international tournament he had left in tears after a 113th minute winning goal from German Mario Götze. But despite it being the scene of his biggest heartbreak, he was determined to come through victorious this time.

Because of Covid restrictions at the time, the Argentinian players had been away from their home and their families for over 40 days in order to compete in the tournament.

40 days away from your family is a very long time, and in a rousing speech to his teammates before kick off, Leo demanded that they make that sacrifice pay off:

"It's been 45 days since we've seen our families! Some of us have missed the birth of our children! But God wanted us to lift this trophy at Maracaná so that it's more beautiful for all of us here. Let's go out there and do it!"

An inspired and resolute Argentina went on to beat Brazil 1-0 in their own back yard.

At full time, all of Leo's teammates embraced him in a sea of joy.

20 years after beginning his football career, he had finally achieved the seemingly impossible: He had finally won a major international trophy for Argentina.

Qatari King

Argentina started the World Cup in Qatar with a 2-1 loss against Saudi Arabia.

In what was widely regarded as being Leo's last ever World Cup, so after that loss, it was feared that the greatest player in the history of the game would leave the international stage with a whimper.

The complete opposite happened after that game. Leo led his young Argentinian team to victory in the next 5 games.

This Argentinian team had grown up as children watching Messi succeed at Barcelona.

Teammates Like Julian Alvarez were born the year Messi moved to Spain, and they had spent their whole childhood watching the best player in the world inspire them to become football players.

They were now being captained by the man himself in a battle to win the greatest trophy in the history of world football.

Argentina reached the final against France on December 18 2022, and what happened in that game will never be forgotten.

It was the most stupendous World Cup final that anyone has, and probably will, ever see.

It was the Mbappe vs Messi show. Two titans of world football battling it out for 120 minutes. Messi scored two goals, Mbappe scored three, and in the end the World Cup had to be decided on penalties.

Messi scored his penalty before it coming down to Gonzalo Montiel to win it for Argentina. When Montiel scored his penalty, Leo collapsed on the floor with tears of happiness flooding his face.

22 years of hard work, sacrifice, setbacks and pain had all just become worth it. He was surrounded by adoring teammates who were also crying with happiness.

They had done it for their family, for their country, and ultimately, for their fearless leader Leo.

At last, Messi had won it all. He had achieved his ultimate goal.

The GOAT

At the time of writing, Messi is still going strong. There is no doubt that he's in the twilight of his career and that he hasn't got many years of playing left.

However, he still has time to add more accolades to a haul that includes:

35 Major trophies at Barcelona
3 Major trophies for Argentina
7 Ballon D'Ors
All time top scorer for Barcelona
All time top scorer for Argentina

The beauty of football, and the reason why we all love the sport, is because it's a game that elicits different emotions and opinions in different people.

The fact is that whether you rank Leo 1st, 2nd or 3rd in the list of all time greats, he is currently the most decorated football player in the history of planet Earth.

He was voted, by his peers, as the best player in the world 7 times. Getting that recognition from your peers is the biggest compliment a football player can be given.

His success is in no doubt due to his enormous determination to overcome any obstacle that has come his way, and it is important to remember that his life was never easy. All his success proves that if you work hard at something, you will get your reward.

And, if you're reading this, you are probably one of the few lucky people to be living in an era where the greatest player ever is still playing football.

So next time he's playing on TV, do yourself a favor and witness poetry in motion. Sit back, relax, and enjoy The Greatest of All Time...

AFA

Made in the USA
Las Vegas, NV
08 December 2023

82328372R00044